Discard

COLD-BLOODED ANIMALS

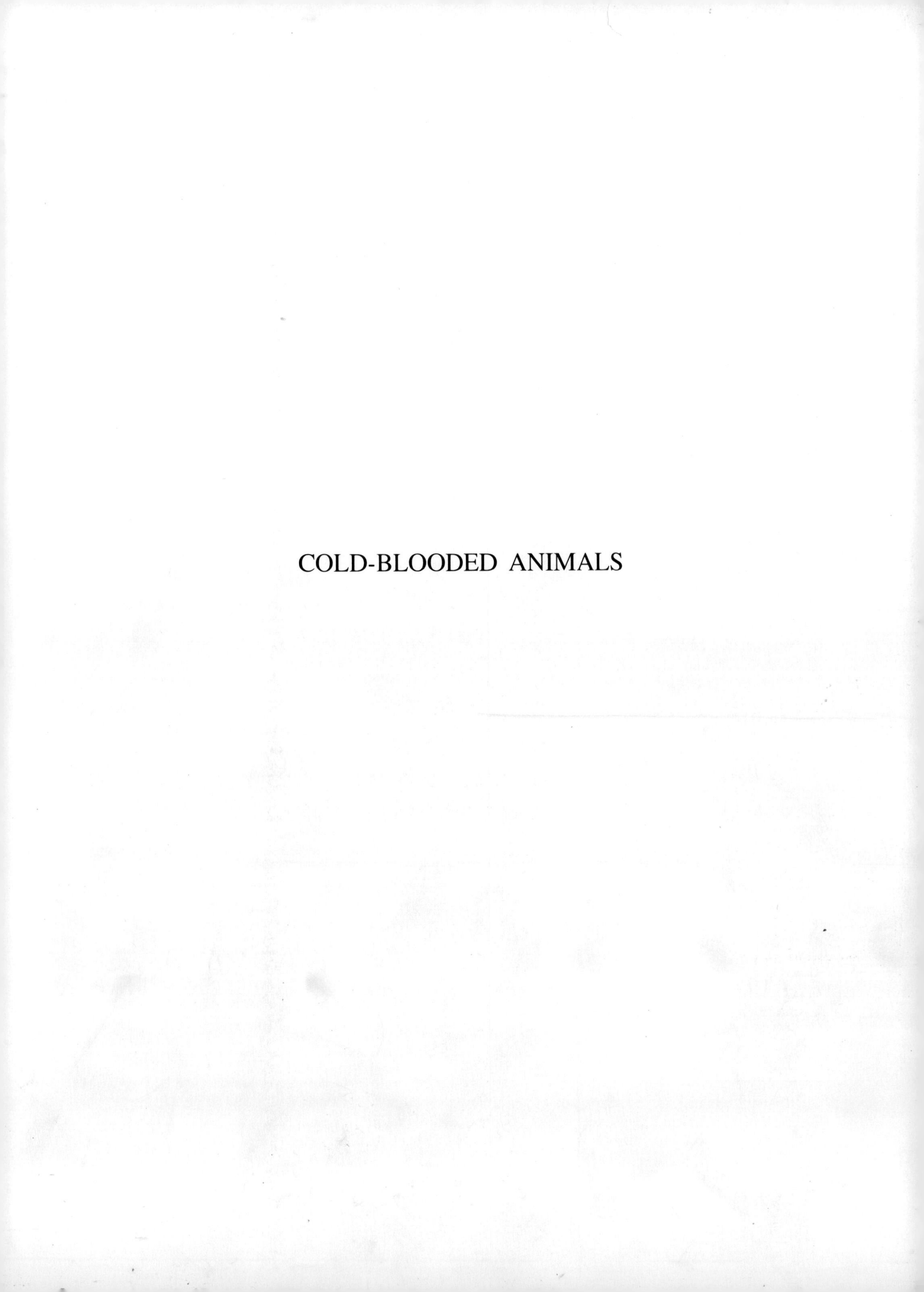

Curriculum Consultants

Dr. Arnold L. Willems
Associate Professor of Curriculum and Instruction
The University of Wyoming

Dr. Gerald W. Thompson
Associate Professor
Social Studies Education
Old Dominion University

Dr. Dale Rice
Associate Professor
Department of Elementary and Early Childhood Education
University of South Alabama

Dr. Fred Finley
Assistant Professor of Science Education
University of Wisconsin

Subject Area Consultants

Astronomy
Robert Burnham
Associate Editor
Astronomy Magazine and *Odyssey* Magazine

Geology
Dr. Norman P. Lasca
Professor of Geology
University of Wisconsin — Milwaukee

Oceanography
William MacLeish
Editor
Oceanus Magazine

Paleontology
Linda West
Dinosaur National Monument
Jensen, Utah

Physiology
Kirk Hogan, M.D.
Madison, Wisconsin

Sociology/Anthropology
Dr. Arnold Willems
Associate Professor of Curriculum and Instruction
College of Education
University of Wyoming

Technology
Dr. Robert T. Balmer
Professor of Mechanical Engineering
University of Wisconsin — Milwaukee

Transportation
James A. Knowles
Division of Transportation
Smithsonian Institution

Irving Birnbaum
Air and Space Museum
Smithsonian Institution

Donald Berkebile
Division of Transportation
Smithsonian Institution

Zoology
Dr. Carroll R. Norden
Professor of Zoology
University of Wisconsin — Milwaukee

First published in Great Britain by Macmillan Children's Books, a division of Macmillan Publishers Ltd, under the title *Look It Up*.
First edition copyright © 1979, 1981 Macmillan Publishers Ltd (for volumes 1-10)
First edition copyright © 1980, 1981 Macmillan Publishers Ltd (for volumes 11-16)
Second edition copyright © 1985, 1986 Macmillan Publishers Ltd

Published in the United States of America

Text this edition copyright © 1986 Raintree Publishers Inc.

All rights reserved. No part of this book may be reproduced or utilized in any form or by any means, electronic or mechanical including photocopying, recording, or by any information storage and retrieval system, without permission in writing from the Publisher. Inquiries should be addressed to Raintree Publishers Inc., 310 West Wisconsin Avenue, Milwaukee, Wisconsin 53202

Library of Congress Number: 86-584

1 2 3 4 5 6 7 8 9 0   90 89 88 87 86

Printed and bound in the United States of America.

Library of Congress Cataloging-in-Publication Data

Let's discover cold-blooded animals.

(Let's discover; 4)
Bibliography: p. 69
Includes index.
Summary: A reference book dealing with cold-blooded animals including octopuses, crabs, spiders, insects, fish, amphibians, and reptiles.
  1. Poikilotherms—Juvenile literature. [1. Cold-blooded animals] I. Title: Cold-blooded animals. II. Series.
AG6.L43 vol. 4, 1986 [QL49] 031s [591] 86-584
ISBN 0-8172-2603-6 (lib. bdg.)
ISBN 0-8172-2484-6 (softcover)

LET'S DISCOVER
COLD-BLOODED ANIMALS

RAINTREE PUBLISHERS
Milwaukee

Contents

COLD-BLOODED ANIMALS — 6

SIMPLE ANIMALS — 8
Animals of the garden — 10
Animals of the rock pool — 12
Octopuses and squids — 14

ANIMALS WITH MANY LEGS — 16
Crabs and lobsters — 18
Shrimps and barnacles — 20
Spiders and scorpions — 22

INSECTS — 24
Butterflies and moths — 26
Flies — 28
Pond animals — 30
Termites — 31
Grasshoppers, crickets, and locusts — 32
Beetles and bugs — 34
Bees, wasps, and ants — 36

FISH — 38
Sharks — 40
Sea fish — 42

River fish	**44**
Unusual fish	**46**

AMPHIBIANS — **48**
Frogs and toads	**50**
Newts and salamanders	**52**

REPTILES — **55**
Lizards	**56**
Crocodiles	**57**
Tortoises and turtles	**58**
Snakes	**60**

ATTACK AND DEFENSE — **62**

GLOSSARY — **64**

FURTHER READING — **69**

QUESTIONS TO THINK ABOUT — **72**

PROJECTS — **79**

INDEX — **80**

COLD-BLOODED ANIMALS

Animals can be divided into two groups. The warm-blooded animals are in one group. The cold-blooded animals are in the other.
Those in the blue circles are cold-blooded. Their body temperatures match their surroundings. Those in the pink circles are warm-blooded. Their temperature stays the same.

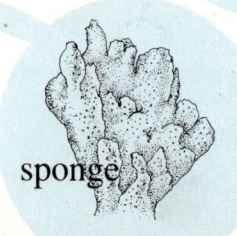

frog

crocodile

fish

sea urchin

starfish

shark

tortoise

jellyfish

sea anemone

worm

coral

snail

octopus

sponge

mussel

bird

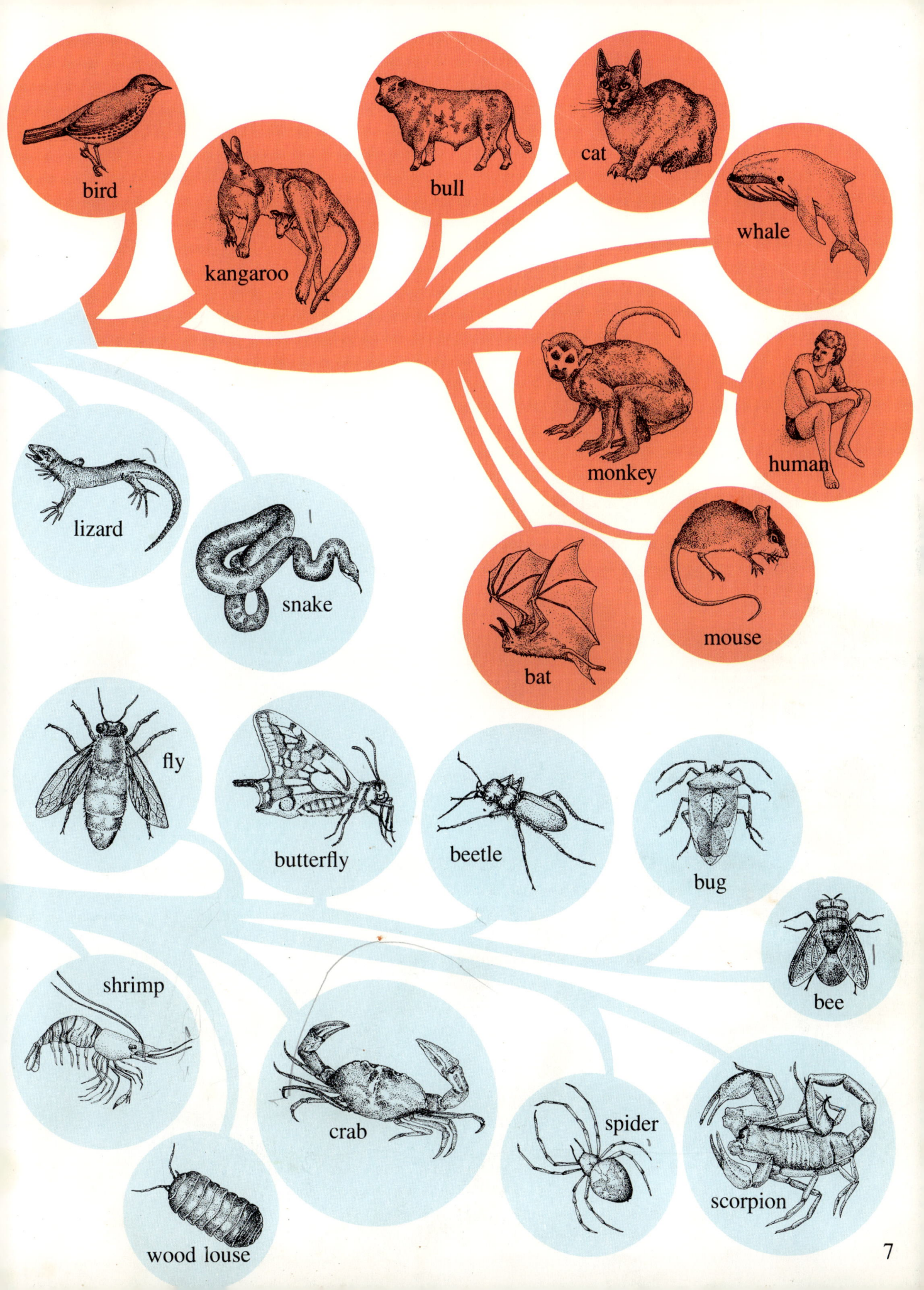

kangaroo

bull

cat

whale

monkey

human

lizard

snake

bat

mouse

fly

butterfly

beetle

bug

bee

shrimp

crab

wood louse

spider

scorpion

7

SIMPLE ANIMALS

Mammals, birds, reptiles, fishes, and amphibians have skeletons of bone. They have a backbone with rows of bones called vertebrae. These animals are called vertebrates. Animals without backbones are called invertebrates. They are simple animals.

The worm the boy is holding is a simple, cold-blooded animal. It is soft. It does not have a skeleton. Its body can bend easily. The crab's body and legs are covered with a hard shell. This is a kind of skeleton.

sea anemone   sponge

The sea anemone has a soft body. Its tentacles sting fish and pull food into its mouth. When the tide is out, the animal closes its mouth to keep wet inside.

Sponges are animals. The bath sponge is really the skeleton of the animal. It is made up of strong fibers. Sponges live mainly in warm, shallow seas.

Animals of the garden

The garden is the home of many simple animals. You can find them on plants, in the earth, or in ponds. Sometimes you must look very carefully. Slugs and snails have soft bodies. They do not like hot, dry weather. When it is hot, snails hide in their shells. Slugs hide in shade.

Earthworms live underground. They come up at night to eat leaves. Moths also come out at night. Most of the animals shown here are seen in daytime. Butterflies and bees fly from flower to flower. Ladybirds and spiders eat other animals. Ants eat honeydew. It is formed by aphids.

white admiral

bumblebee

honeybees

large heath butterfly

peacock butterfly

wasps

garden snail

11

Animals of the rock pool

The seashore is a good place to look for animals. When the tide goes out, sea creatures are left in rock pools. Can you see the prawns and blennies swimming in this pool? Sea anemones, mussels, and barnacles stick to the rocks. Limpets and topshells crawl around slowly.

The giant clam lives on coral reefs. It grows to one meter (39 in) across and can weigh 250 kilograms (550 lbs).

barnacles

prawns

blenny

Starfish live in the sea. Sometimes they come into rock pools. They eat shellfish.

limpets

barnacles

mussels

sea anemones

blenny

topshells

13

Octopuses and squids

All mollusks have soft bodies. Mollusks such as winkles, clams, and limpets are protected by hard shells. They move slowly. Octopuses and squids are mollusks that do not have shells. They live in the sea. They can move very fast. Their long arms have rows of suckers. The suckers catch their food.

octopus

An octopus has eight arms. It walks on the sea bed, or swims by squirting a jet of water. Its poisonous bite kills its prey.

A squid has ten arms. It also moves by squirting a jet of water. The jet moves the squid forward. Giant squids grow to 20 meters (65 ft) in length. This giant squid is fighting with a whale.

giant squid

sperm whale

ANIMALS WITH MANY LEGS

Most animals with backbones have four legs or fins. Some stand upright on their back legs. Others use their tail as a kind of third leg. Animals without backbones have many other sets of legs. Some animals have no legs at all.

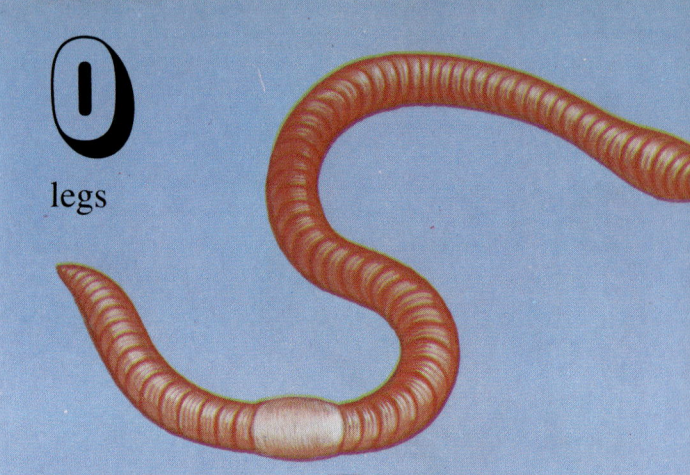

0 legs

A worm has no legs. It moves by pushing out its head and then pulling its body forward.

1 leg

A snail crawls on its stomach, which is a kind of foot. It lays a sticky trail that helps it slide.

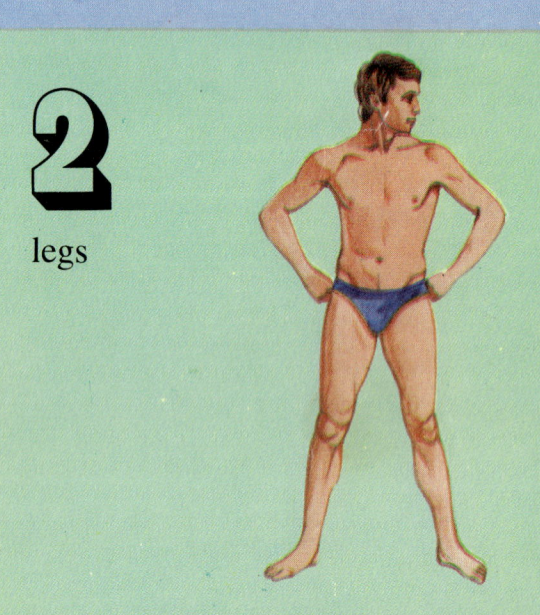

2 legs

People stand upright on two legs.

3 — two legs and a tail

Kangaroos use a tail for balance.

4 legs

Bears walk on all four legs.

16

5 four legs and a tail

This monkey uses its tail as a fifth leg. This helps it move through the trees.

6 legs

The six-legged mantis is an insect. It catches food with its front legs.

8 legs

Spiders have eight legs. The extra pair of legs makes spiders different from insects.

10 legs

Crabs have ten legs. The front legs are claws.

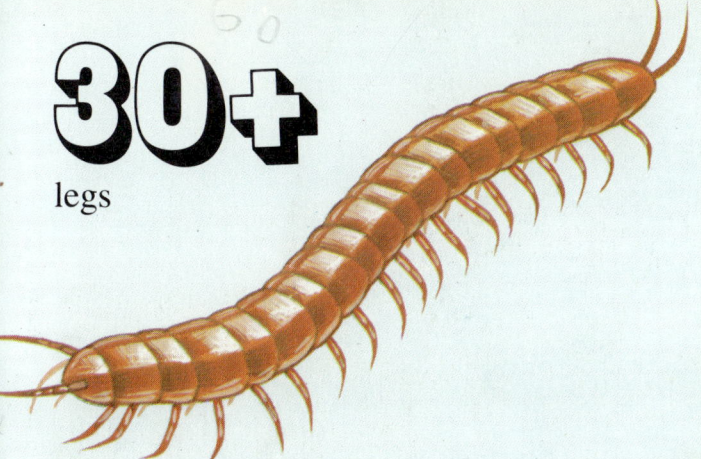

30+ legs

A centipede has one pair of legs on each section of its body.

60+ legs

A millipede has two pairs of legs on each section of its body.

17

Crabs and lobsters

Crabs and lobsters are called crustaceans. Their bodies are covered with an outside skeleton. This is their shell. As they grow, they shed their old shell and grow a new one. They have five pairs of legs. The two front legs are large claws. They are used for fighting and for catching food. Most crabs and lobsters live in the sea.

The shore crab is often seen in rock pools and on beaches. It eats any animals it can catch with its claws. It defends itself with its claws. If you pick up a shore crab, it may nip you.

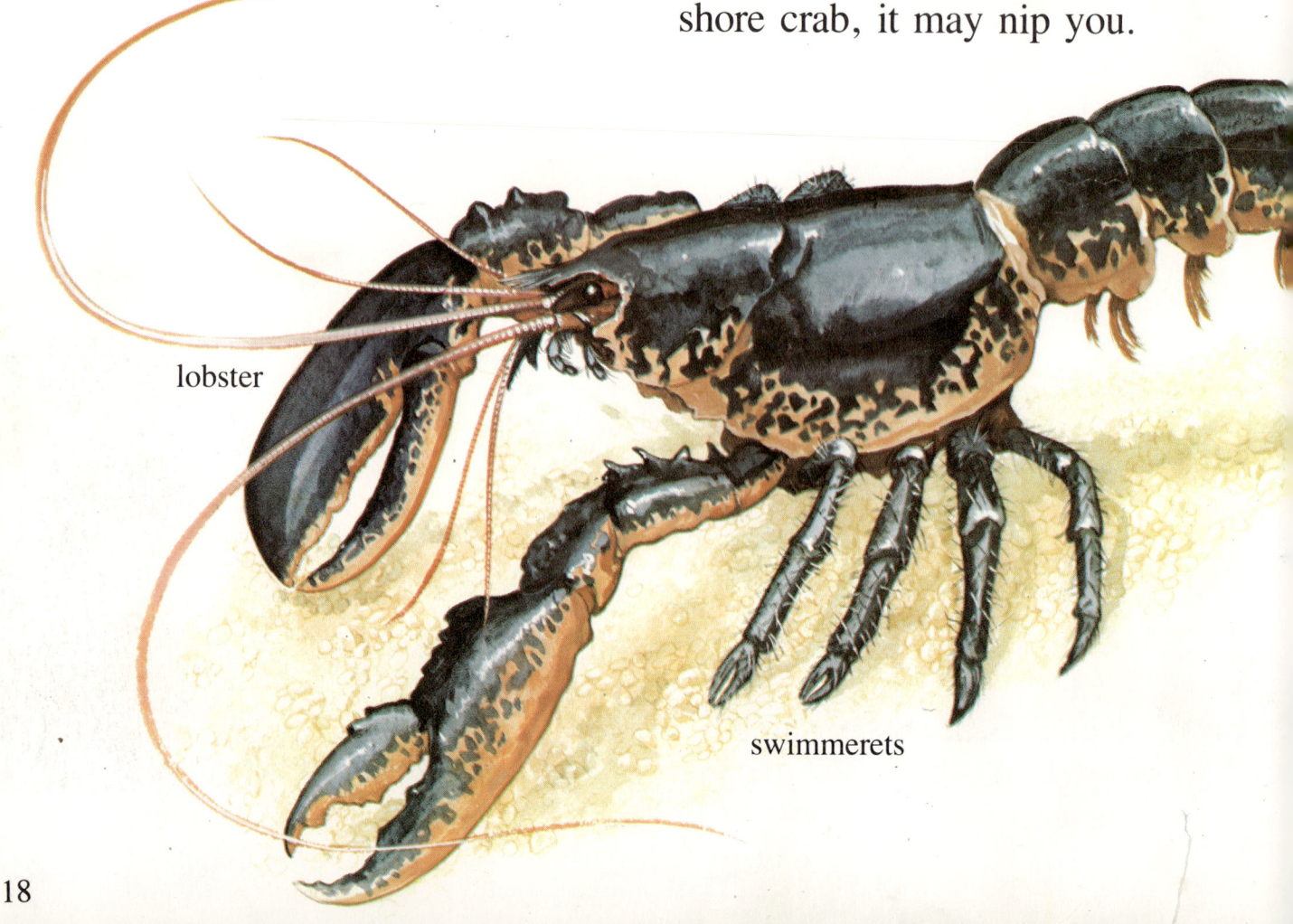

lobster

swimmerets

Fiddler crabs have one big claw.
They use it to signal other crabs.
Fiddler crabs are found
near the shore.

Lobsters have very long bodies.
They have several pairs of legs
that they use for swimming. They
are called swimmerets. Fishermen
catch lobsters in pots like the one
on the right. The lobster enters
the pot to get food.

19

Shrimps and barnacles

Shrimps and barnacles are both crustaceans. But they look very different. A shrimp looks like a tiny lobster. It can swim very well. A barnacle looks like a limpet. When it is covered with water, its hard shell opens. Pieces of food wash into its mouth when it waves its legs around.

Baby barnacles float in the sea. When they are older, they fix themselves to something solid. They usually stick to rocks. Sometimes they stick to ships. In the picture above, you can see men scraping barnacles off the side of a ship.

This shrimp is living in a clam shell. It is safe from its enemies. It comes out only to feed.

When the tide goes out, barnacles shut their shells. They are safe until the tide comes in again. Shrimps that are trapped in rock pools are easy to catch.

Spiders and scorpions

All insects have six legs. Spiders and scorpions have eight legs. So they are not insects. Scorpions have a front pair of claws. They have long bodies, and their tails have a sting in the tip. Spiders have round bodies.

scorpion

Scorpions use their claws to catch food. They use their sting only to defend themselves.

This spider has caught a fly in its web and is wrapping it in silk. The fly is its food.

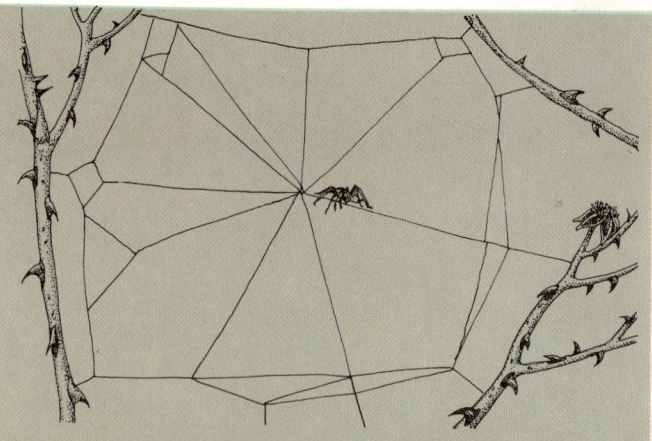

To build a web, the spider first makes a frame of silk threads.

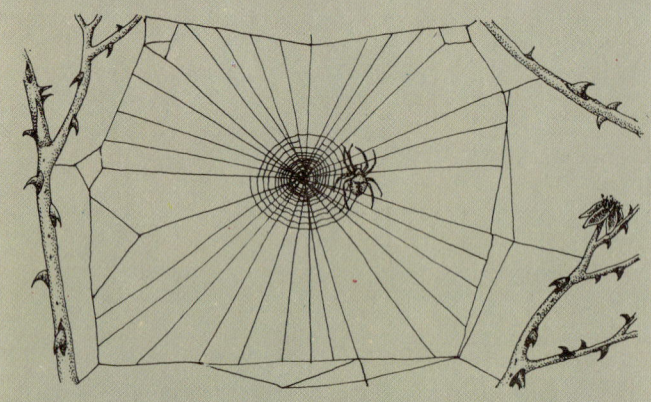

Next, the spider lays rings of silk threads on the frame.

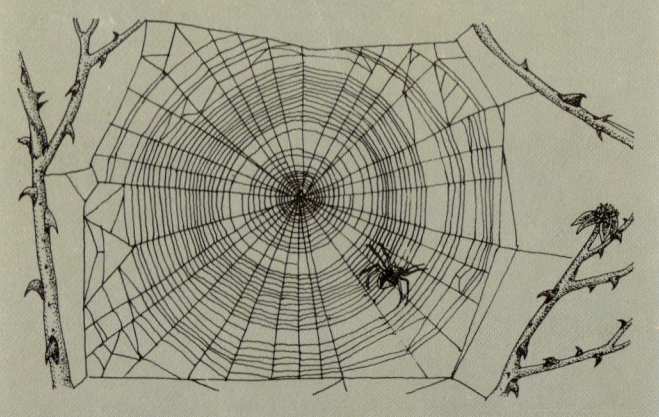

When the web is finished, the spider sits and waits for flies to be trapped in it.

This spider is waiting patiently in its web. When a fly is caught by the sticky silk, it struggles. This struggling warns the spider. It runs across the web and kills the fly with its poison bite.

INSECTS

You can recognize an insect easily. It has six legs and its body has three parts. Most insects lay eggs. But some give birth to baby insects. Some young insects look like their parents. They are called nymphs. Others have soft, worm-like bodies. They are called caterpillars. They change into adults inside a case called a pupa.

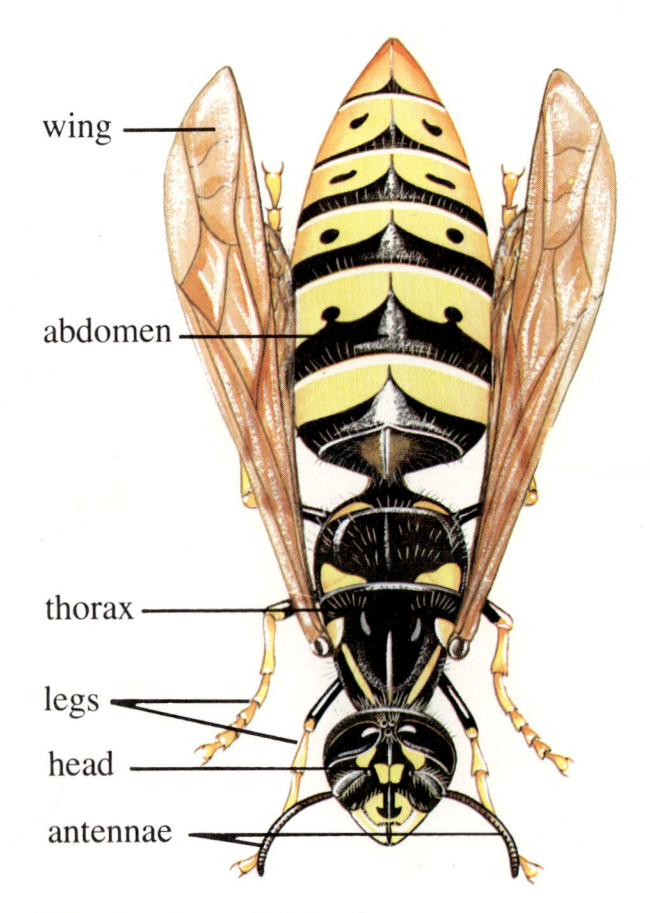

The life of a butterfly or moth starts with an egg. You can often find insect eggs on leaves.

wing
abdomen
thorax
legs
head
antennae

The body of this insect, a wasp, has a head, a thorax, and an abdomen. The wings and legs are joined to the thorax.

When a pupa splits open, the adult butterfly or moth crawls out. Adults do not live long.

The egg hatches into a caterpillar. The caterpillar spends most of its time eating. It grows very fast.

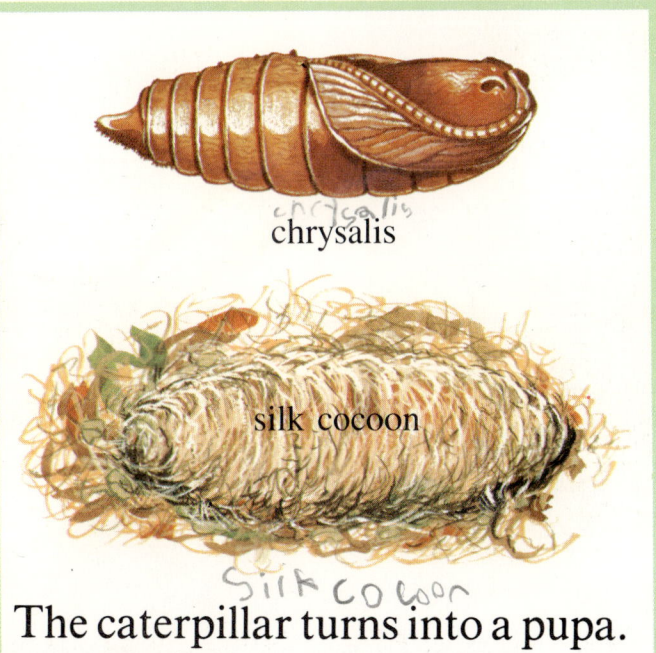

chrysalis

silk cocoon

The caterpillar turns into a pupa. A butterfly pupa is called a chrysalis. Moths spin a silk cocoon.

Butterflies and moths

The wings of butterflies and moths are covered with tiny scales. They are often brightly colored. The best way to tell a butterfly from a moth is to look at its antennae. A butterfly's antennae end in knobs. A moth usually has feathery antennae.

garden tiger moth

Most moths fly at night and hide by day. The garden tiger moth cannot hide well. It is too colorful. The elephant hawk moth only comes out on warm summer nights.

The bull's-eye moth in the picture above has spots like eyes on its wings. These spots scare away birds that eat moths. Most moths have wings that fasten together with a tiny hook. Butterflies have no hooks.

elephant hawk moth

emperor moth

monarch butterfly

swallowtail butterfly

common blue butterfly

peacock butterfly

Butterflies do not look like strong fliers. But some kinds go long distances. The monarch butterfly of America flies 3,000 kilometers (1864 mi) to spend the winter in warm countries. Sometimes it flies across the Atlantic. Swallowtails and blue butterflies stay in one place.

Brazilian skipper butterfly

Many insects die at the end of the summer. Peacock butterflies are different. They live in hollow trees and in buildings during the winter. In spring, they wake up and fly away. You can see them in many different places. They live in parks, gardens, and forests.

Flies

Most insects have two pairs of wings. Flies have only one pair. Instead of the rear pair of wings, they have two tiny stalks. The stalks help them to balance when flying. Some flies are dangerous. They carry germs that cause disease. Some mosquitoes spread a disease called malaria.

We must never let houseflies walk on food in the kitchen or stores.

The picture shows a long-legged cranefly. Its long, thin legs break off easily. The grubs of craneflies are called leather-jackets. They live underground.

Flies carry germs on their feet. Germs cause disease. When you eat the food, you eat the germs.

The germs soon make you sick. So always cover food. It is best to keep food in a refrigerator.

Hover flies look like wasps, but they cannot sting you. They can hover and fly backward, just like a helicopter.

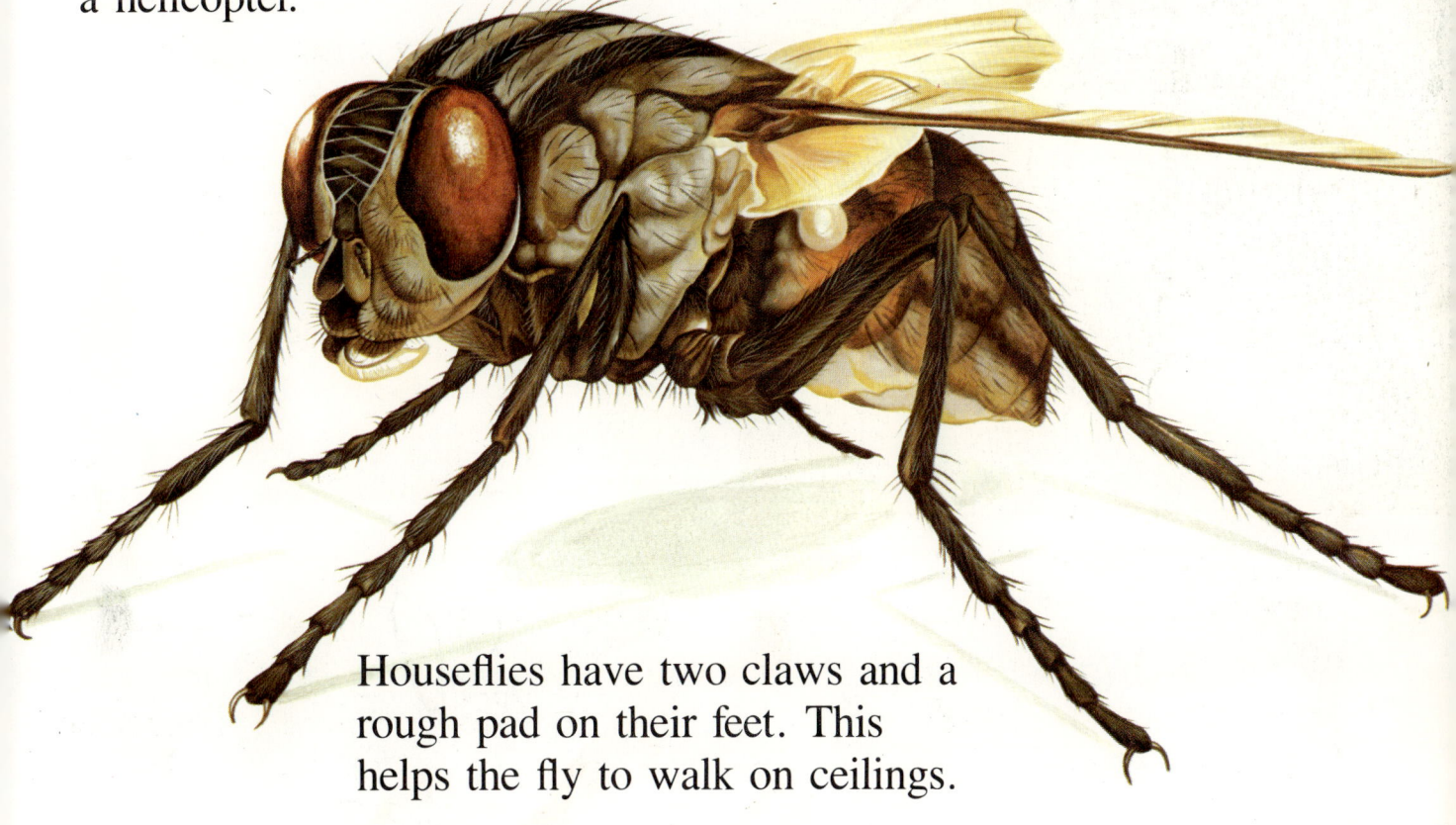

Houseflies have two claws and a rough pad on their feet. This helps the fly to walk on ceilings.

Pond animals

Some kinds of insects live in ponds. Dragonflies lay their eggs in pond water. The water beetle and the water boatman live in ponds. Many pond insects eat other animals. You can see a baby dragonfly, called a dragonfly larva, in this picture. It eats the larva of the other pond animals.

dragonfly

damselfly

great water beetle

water boatman

water beetle larva

dragonfly larva

mayfly larva

caddisfly larva

Termites

Termites live in large nests, such as the one on the right. These nests are like castles made of hard earth. The nests can be as high as five meters (16 ft). Termites live in warm places, in Australia and parts of the Americas. Their main food is wood. They attack wooden buildings.

A termite nest is the home of a queen termite, a king, and thousands of worker termites. The queen grows up to five centimeters (almost 2 in) long. All she does is eat and lay eggs.

queen termite

Grasshoppers, crickets, and locusts

Grasshoppers and crickets have long back legs. They are good jumpers. They also have wings and can fly. These insects usually come out in warm weather. You can see grasshoppers in the daytime. Crickets mostly come out at night.

The skins of insects cannot stretch. As they grow, they shed their old skins and grow new ones that are larger. This grasshopper is climbing out of its old skin.

Locusts live in hot countries. Sometimes they form big groups called swarms. People may call these swarms 'plagues.' Young locusts are called hoppers. They cannot fly. Like the adults, they can destroy crops.

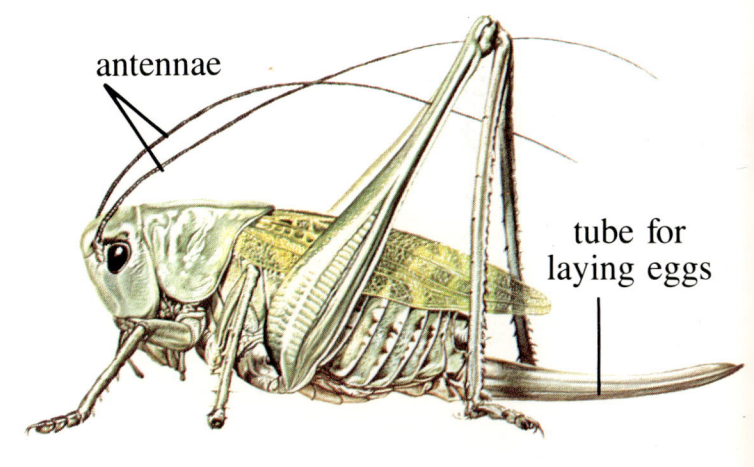

antennae

tube for laying eggs

Crickets have longer antennae than grasshoppers have. This female has a long tube at the end of her body. She pushes it into the earth and lays eggs through it.

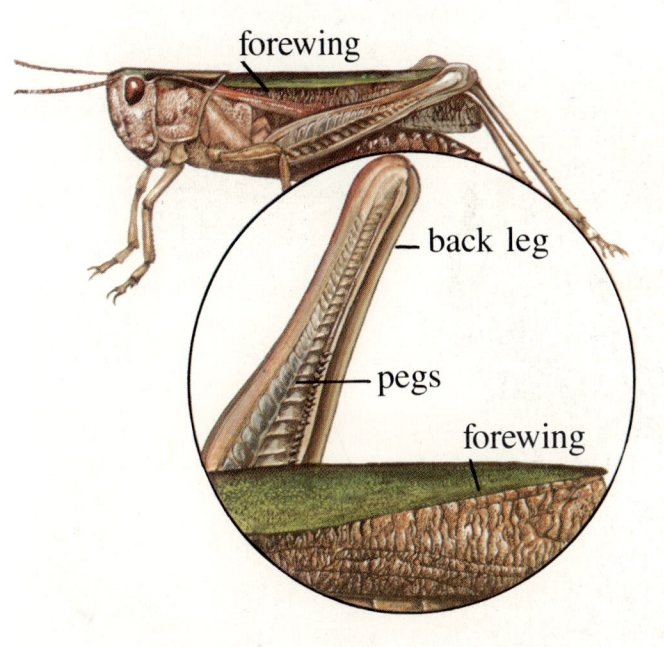

forewing

back leg

pegs

forewing

A grasshopper's back leg has a row of pegs on one side. It makes a buzzing sound by rubbing these pegs against its forewing.

Beetles and bugs

Beetles are insects that have hard front wing cases. They are often brightly colored. These protect the soft back wings. A bug is also an insect. It has six legs and a three-part body. Its mouth has a hollow tube. The tube has a sharp tip and is used for sucking up food.

aphids

Aphids are bugs that suck the sap from plants. They can hurt gardens. So gardeners get rid of aphids and other bugs.

The large picture shows two stag beetles. Their big jaws look like the antlers of a stag, or male deer. These stag beetles are using their jaws for fighting.

stag beetles

This ladybug is taking off from a plant. You can see its brightly colored front wings.

Ladybugs are beetles. They eat aphids and other bugs.

backswimmer

The backswimmer or water boatman always swims on its back. It rows along with its back legs. It sucks the blood of other animals. If you touch one, it might sting your finger.

35

Bees, wasps, and ants

Bees, wasps, and ants are insects that live in large nests. In each nest, there is a queen that lays eggs. The eggs hatch into grubs. Worker insects look after the nest and find food. In summer, new young queens mate with males and fly away to start new nests.

A crowd of worker bees, called a swarm, goes away with each queen.

A worker wasp eats fruit. It also catches insects for the grubs.

swarm

drone

worker

queen

The honeybees that you see flying from flower to flower are workers. They get nectar and pollen from flowers to make into honey. They have a sting that they use to defend the nest. The queen and male bees, called drones, only leave the nest when they mate.

Worker ants do not have wings, as do bees and wasps. They must walk when looking for food. They are very small. But they are strong. They can easily carry food a long way back to the nest. The parasol ant in the picture is taking a flower to its nest. Parasol ants eat a fungus that grows on the flower.

FISH

Fish are the oldest animals with backbones that we find today. Nearly all fish live in water. Lungfish and some others can stay on land for a short time. Fish swim by moving their tails. Fins help them to keep their balance and to steer. Their bodies are covered with scales.

Most fish lay eggs. A few give birth to baby fish. Some fish protect their eggs until hatching.

A fish needs oxygen to breathe. It gets oxygen from water. The fish takes water into its mouth. Its gills take oxygen from the water and squirt the water out.

You can keep fish in a tank of water called an aquarium. Rocks and weeds make the aquarium look like a pond.

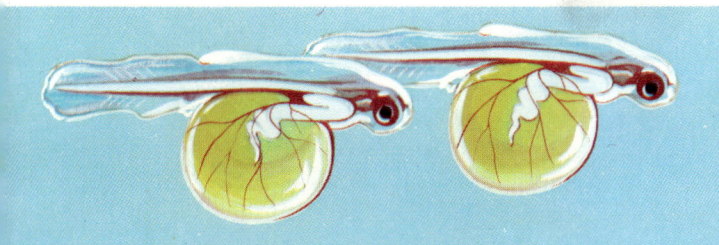

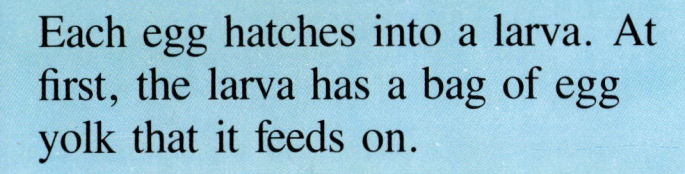

Each egg hatches into a larva. At first, the larva has a bag of egg yolk that it feeds on.

The yolk disappears as the fish grows up. This fully grown fish has fins and a tail.

fish in aquarium

Sharks

Sharks are fish that have a skeleton made of soft cartilage instead of bone. Most sharks have sharp teeth. They eat other fish. Great white sharks are fierce hunters. They sometimes eat people. Blue sharks and leopard sharks also may attack people.

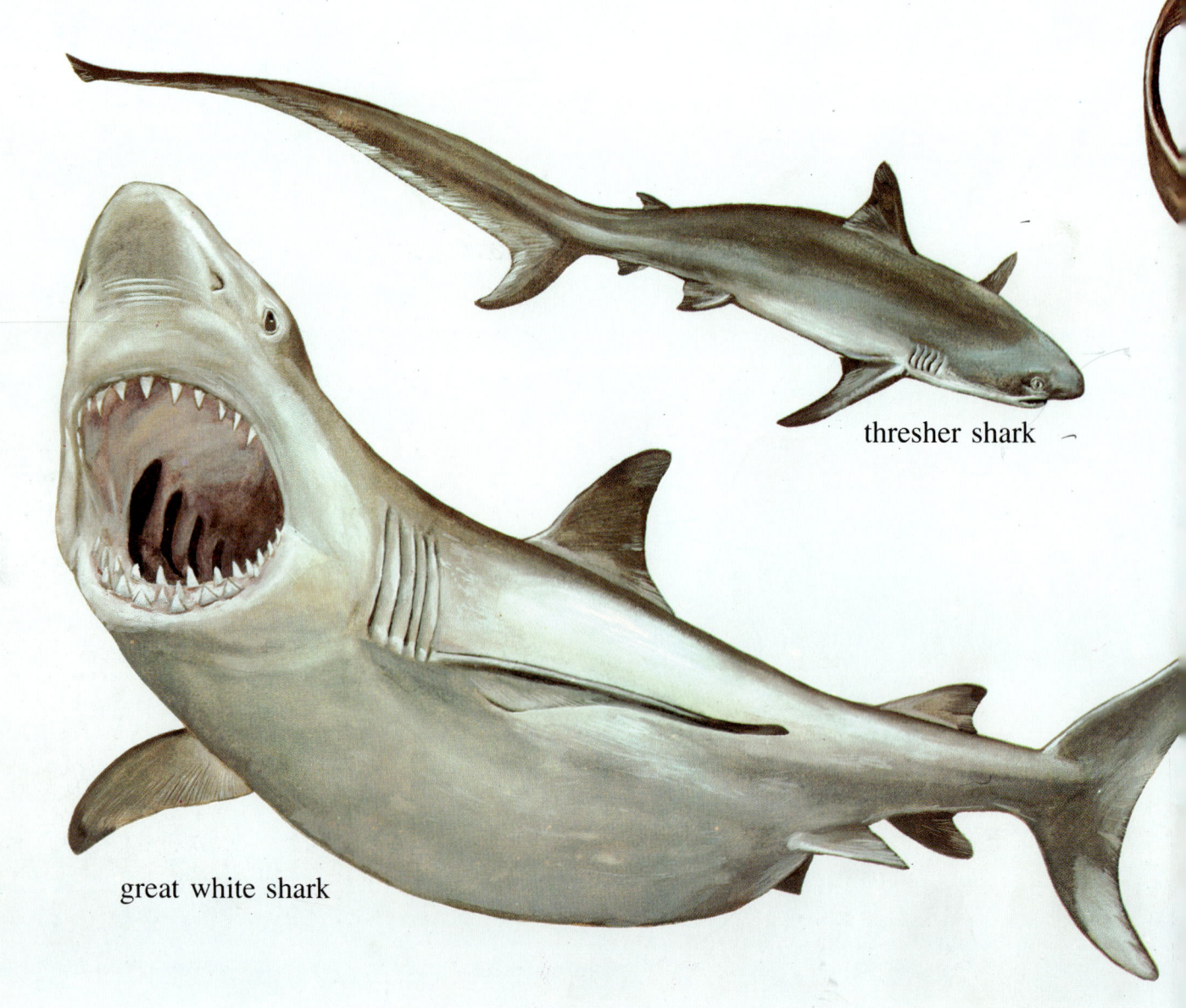

blue shark

thresher shark

great white shark

leopard shark

hammerhead shark

Sharks may be a danger to divers. So divers carry weapons. But sharks do not usually attack, as the picture shows.

Some sharks have baby sharks. Others lay eggs in cases called mermaid purses.

Sea fish

The coral reefs of warm seas are the homes of many amazing fish. Many of them have bright colors. Some of the fish that live in coral reefs are dangerous. The lionfish has a nasty sting. The moray eel has sharp teeth and sometimes bites divers.

sea horse

scorpion fish

clown fish

puffer fish

angel fish

butterfly fish

batfish

sea anemone

moray eel

43

River fish

These are fish that live in lakes and rivers. Some are good to eat. The brown trout lives in clear streams. It eats insects that land on the water. The eel leaves the river and swims to sea when it is grown up. The pike is a fierce hunter. It eats other fish.

kingfisher

pike

barbel

dace

brown trout

dace

chub

eel

tench

45

Unusual fish

There are thousands of different kinds of fish. Many look very strange. Some have odd habits. Some fish can glide through the air. Others can climb trees.

Surgeon fish, such as the one in the top picture, live in coral reefs. They have a bone near the tail that is as sharp as a surgeon's knife.

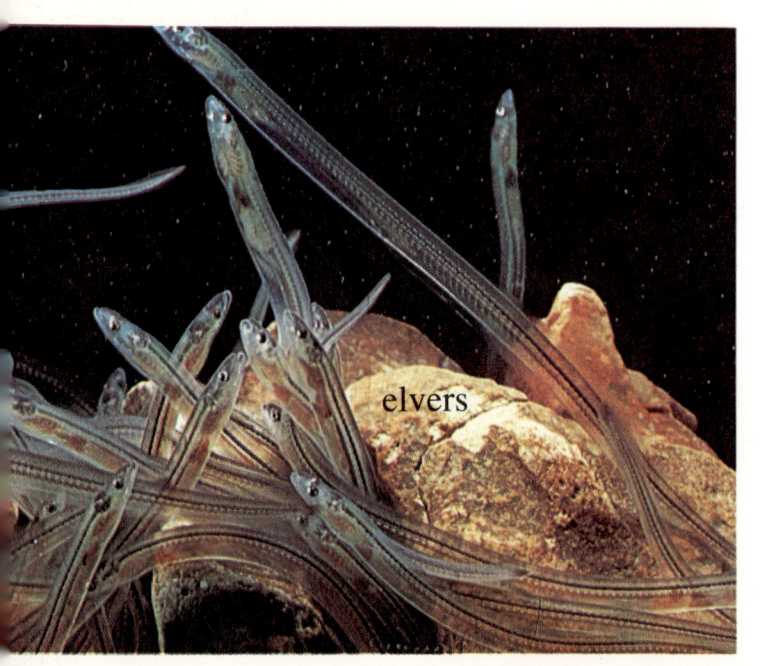

elvers

Baby eels are called elvers. Elvers swim thousands of kilometers from the warm sea where they hatch. They swim to the rivers of North America and Europe.

sea horse.

The sea horse swims by moving the fin on its back. The female lays her eggs in a pouch on the male's belly. On hatching, the babies swim out.

On the left is a puffer fish. It can blow up its body like a balloon. This makes it too big for its enemies to swallow.

AMPHIBIANS

Amphibians are animals that can live either on land or in water. Their eggs do not have shells. They must be laid in water. The adult's skin must be kept wet. But a few amphibians do live in dry places.

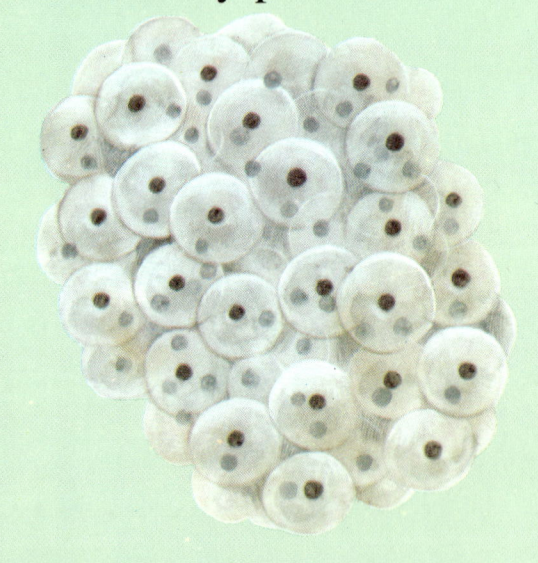

tiny tadpoles

Frogs are amphibians. Their eggs are covered with jelly. The jelly protects the eggs.

You can see the eggs changing into tadpoles. It takes two weeks from laying to hatching.

At first, the tadpole has no legs. It looks like a fish, and it breathes with gills.

two days old

six days old

In the picture above, you see a tadpole six days after hatching.

On the left, you see clumps of frog eggs in a pond. The parent frog leaves the eggs as soon as they are laid.

As the tadpole grows bigger, it starts to grow legs. The back legs grow first. The front legs are hidden by gill flaps.

six weeks old

eight weeks old

After twelve weeks, the tadpole begins to look like a frog. Its tail starts to shrink.

twelve weeks old

The adult frog has no tail. It hops on its legs. It has lungs.

Most amphibians lay eggs that hatch into tadpoles. The tadpoles look very different from their parents. They live in water and slowly change into adults. Then they leave the water and live on land. When they are fully grown, they return to water to lay eggs.

adult frog

Frogs and toads

Frogs and toads are amphibians without tails. The largest is the goliath frog of Africa. It is 30 centimeters (1 ft) long. Frogs and toads hop on land and swim in water. Frogs have smoother skins and longer legs than toads.

Frogs and toads sing by making croaks and grunts. The reed frog shown below puffs up its throat when it sings.

This male toad carries eggs from the female on his legs. He must keep the eggs wet.

Tree frogs live in hot countries. They climb well and jump from branch to branch. Their green color matches their surroundings.

Newts and salamanders

Newts and salamanders also are amphibians. But they do not lose their tails when they grow up. They look like lizards, but they have a wet skin. When they run, they wiggle their body from side to side. Like other amphibians, they eat small animals.

Fire salamanders, such as the one you see below, live in Europe. People once thought fire salamanders could walk through fire without being burned. But this is not true.

The giant salamander lives in North America. It climbs trees. It barks when alarmed.

The axolotl shown at the right is a salamander that never grows up. It spends its whole life as a tadpole.

When the time comes to lay eggs, newts gather in ponds. The male newts, such as the one shown below, become brightly colored.

Australian rock python

The Australian rock python curls around her eggs until they hatch. She protects her eggs from her enemies in this way.

REPTILES

Reptiles are animals that have a dry skin covered with scales. Most reptiles spend all of their lives on land. Their eggs have a leathery covering. They are laid on land. The eggs of some reptiles hatch inside the mother's body, so baby reptiles are born.

Millions of years ago, giant reptiles called dinosaurs were very important land animals.

lizard

The tuatara shown above is an ancient reptile. It looks like a lizard. It lives on islands near New Zealand.

Like all reptiles, lizards are cold-blooded. They warm their bodies by lying in the sun, as the one on the left is doing. They can run fast when they are warm. At night, lizards hide under rocks.

Lizards

Lizards are reptiles with thin bodies and tails. But the shingle-back lizard is fatter than other lizards. One kind, the frilled dragon, runs on its back legs. The goanna has strong claws. The gecko has special pads on its feet, so it can stick to walls.

legless lizard

shingle-back lizard

leaf-tailed gecko

spotted goanna

frilled dragon

Crocodiles

Crocodiles live near water. They swim well. Some kinds live in the sea. They usually eat fish. But they can kill large animals by drowning them. Crocodiles may grow to eight meters (26 ft) long. But they are becoming rare. Alligators and gharials are two kinds of crocodiles.

American alligator

gharial

Siamese crocodile

Tortoises and turtles

Tortoises and turtles are reptiles with hard shells. Some kinds can pull their head and legs into the shell for safety. Tortoises live on land. Turtles live in water. A turtle's legs are flippers that it uses for swimming. It lays its eggs on land.

This giant tortoise can carry a boy on its back. Some giant tortoises live for 150 years.

The green turtle lives in the sea. It eats a kind of grass that grows on the sea bed. Turtles come ashore to lay their eggs.

turtle

Tortoises grow very slowly. They live for a long time. They cannot walk very fast. But they can protect themselves by pulling in their head and legs. These animals usually eat plants. But sometimes they eat slugs and worms.

tortoises

terrapin

Terrapins are small turtles. They live in freshwater ponds and rivers.

Snakes

Snakes are reptiles without legs. They eat other animals. They can open their mouths very wide to swallow large animals. Some are poisonous. Others squeeze their prey to death.

Snakes are deaf. They do not hear the snake charmer's music. They sway in time to his movements.

This game of snakes and ladders shows some colorful snakes.

California king snake

adder

scarlet snake

cobra

gaboon viper

green mamba

rattlesnake

garter snake

61

ATTACK AND DEFENSE

Cold-blooded animals have many different ways of harming their enemies. Bees and wasps sting to defend themselves. Poisonous snakes bite when they cannot escape. Some animals attack to get food. Animals that suck blood can spread diseases. Mosquitoes can do this.

Jellyfish sting small animals, which they then eat.

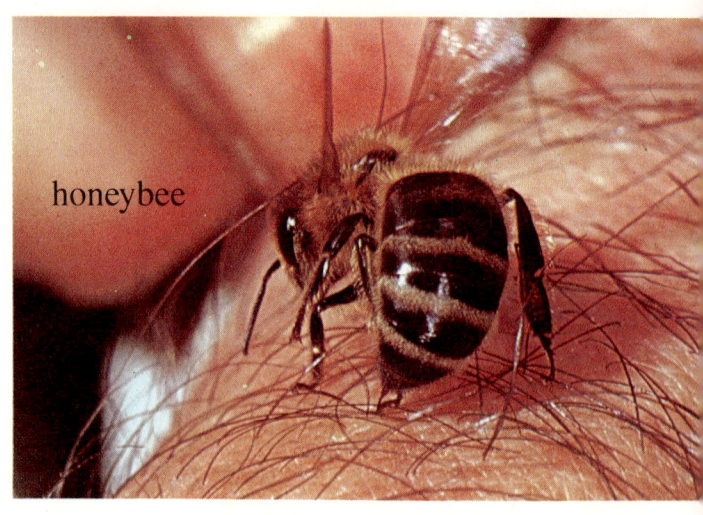

The sting of the honeybee sends poison through a tube at the tip of the bee's body.

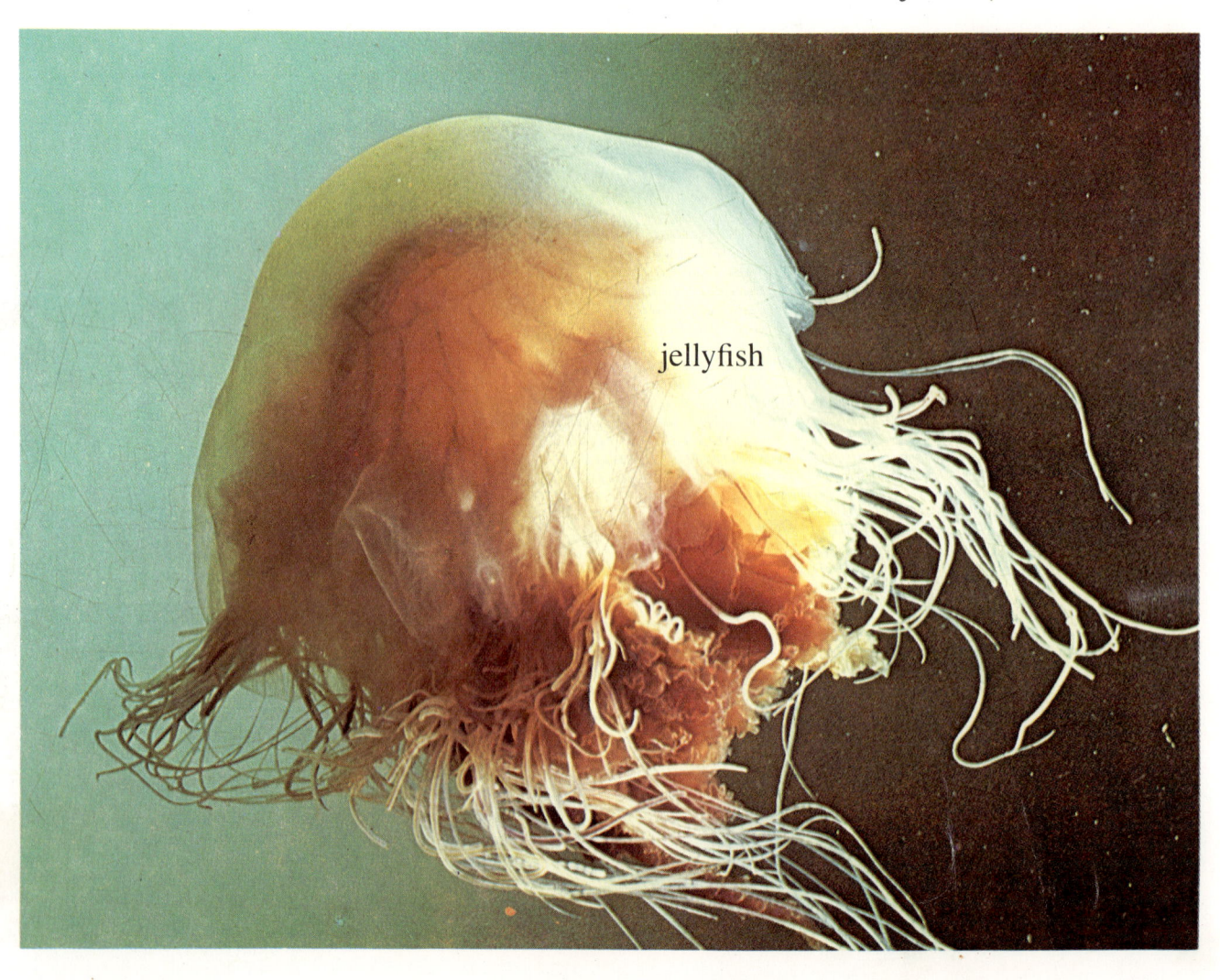

leech

Leeches stick to the skin of an animal and suck its blood.

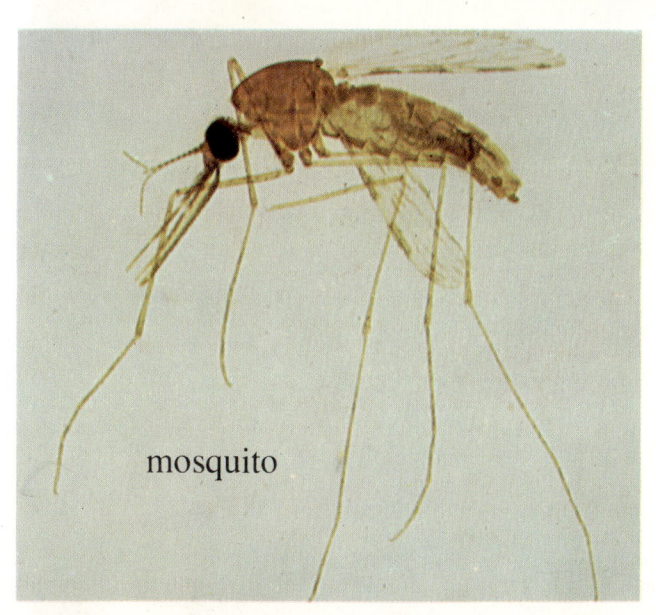

mosquito

Mosquitoes suck blood through a hollow tube. They spread diseases.

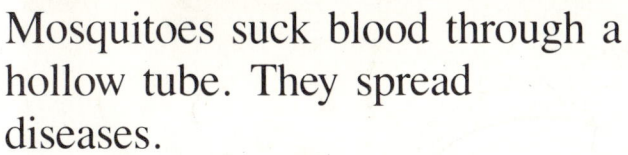

Piranhas are small fish. They attack and eat large animals that wade or swim in the river.

piranha

63

GLOSSARY

These words are defined the way they are used in the book.

abdomen (AB duh muhn) the end part of an insect's body

alligator (AL ih GAY tur) a type of crocodile

amphibian (am FIB ee uhn) a cold-blooded animal that can live either on land or in water

antennae (an TEN ee) a pair of long feelers on the head of an insect

aphid (AY fihd) a tiny bug that sucks the sap from plants

aquarium (uh KWAIR ee uhm) a tank where fish and other water animals are kept

axolotl (AX oh LOH t'l) a salamander that grows into the tadpole stage but never grows out of it

back swimmer (BAK swih mur) another name for a water boatman

barnacle (BAHR nuk k'l) a crustacean that sticks to rocks or boats

beetle (beet'l) an insect with hard shiny front wings

blenny (BLEH nee) a small fish with spikey fins that lives in rock pools by the seashore

bull's eye moth (bools aye mawth) a moth with spots like eyes on its wings

butterfly (BUH tur fly) an insect with brightly colored wings and antennae with a knob on the ends

butterfly fish (BUH tur fly fihsh) a fish with a tall fin and brightly colored skin that makes it look like a butterfly

camouflage (CAM oo flahzh) a disguise or false appearance that is used to help hide an animal

caterpillar (CA tur pihl ahr) a baby insect with a soft, worm-like body

centipede (SEHN tuh peed) a worm-like animal with one pair of legs on each section of its body

chrysalis (KRIH sa lihs) a butterfly pupa

clownfish (KLOWN fihsh) a fish that is brightly colored like a clown's face

cocoon (kuh KOON) the silk case where a caterpillar changes into a moth

cold-blooded (KOHLD bluhd ihd) having blood that stays the same temperature as the air and surfaces around it

coral reef (KAWR uhl reef) a pile of hard substance that is left after tiny sea animals die

crab (krab) a simple animal with

10 legs and a hard shell

cricket (KRIH keht) a short-legged hopping insect

crocodile (KRAHK uh dyl) a large reptile that lives near water and is a good swimmer

crustacean (kruhs TAY shuhn) an invertebrate with a hard skin that protects it

dinosaur (DY nuh sawr) a large reptile that lived a long time ago

dragonfly (DRAG uhn fly) a long, thin flying insect

drone (drohn) a male bee

earthworm (URTH wurm) a long, thin simple animal that lives underground and comes out at night to eat leaves

eel (eel) a long, skinny fish

elver (EHL vur) a baby eel

emperor moth (EHM pur awr mawth) a moth with spots like eyes on its wings

fiddler crab (FIHD lur krab) a crustacean with one huge claw

flipper (FLIH pur) a broad flat limb used for swimming and moving on land

forewing (FAWR wihng) an insect's front wing

frilled dragon (FRIHLD DRA guhn) a lizard with a ruffle of skin around its head; it runs on its back legs

gecko (GEH koh) a lizard with special pads on its feet so it can hold on to walls

gharial (GHAIR ee ahl) a type of crocodile

gill (gihl) part of a fish used for breathing

goanna (GOH ah na) a lizard with strong, curved claws

goliath frog (GOH ly ath frawg) the largest frog in the world; it lives in Africa

grasshopper (GRAHS haw pur) an insect with long back legs for jumping

hopper (HAW pur) a young locust that cannot fly

hover fly (HUHV ur fly) a wasp-like insect that can fly backwards

insect (IHN sehkt) a simple animal; its body is divided into three parts and it has six legs

invertebrate (ihn VUR tuh briht) an animal without a backbone, also called a simple animal

jellyfish (JEL ee fihsh) a soft-bodied sea animal

kingfisher (KIHNG fihsh ur) a brightly colored bird that eats small fish

ladybug (LAY dee buhg) a red-winged beetle that eats other bugs

larva (LAHR vuh) a young fish or insect

leather-jacket (LEH thur ja keht) a baby crane fly

legless lizard (LEHG lehs LIH zahrd) a lizard that crawls like a snake

leech (leech) a long, thin animal that attaches its mouth to an animal and sucks its blood

leopard shark (LEH pahrd shahrk) a shark with spots on its skin

limpet (LIHM peht) a mollusk that moves slowly and has a hard shell

lionfish (LY uhn fihsh) a fish with a sting

lizard (LIH zahrd) a cold-blooded animal with a long, slim body, tail and short feet

lobster (LAHB stur) a crustacean with a long body, several pairs of legs and two large claws

locust (LOH kuhst) a type of grasshopper

lungfish (LUHNG fihsh) a fish that can breathe out of water for a short time

mammal (MAM uhl) a warm-blooded animal that feeds its young on the mother's milk

mantis (MAHN tihs) an insect that catches food with its front legs

mermaid purse (MUR mayd purs) a shark's egg

millipede (MIH lih peed) a worm-like animal with two pairs of legs on each section of its body

mollusk (MAWL uhsk) a simple animal with a soft body and no bones

monarch butterfly (MAWN ahrk BUH tur fly) a butterfly that travels to warm countries in the winter

moray eel (MAHR ay eel) a long fish with sharp teeth that lives in coral reefs

mosquito (muhs KEE toh) a flying insect that sucks blood when it bites

mussel (mus'l) a mollusk with a hard shell

newt (noot) an amphibian that looks like a lizard with a long tail but has damp skin

nymph (nihmf) a baby insect that looks just like its parent

octopus (AWK tuh pus) a mollusk with eight arms and no shell

parasol ant (PAIR uh sawl ant) an ant that carries its food, a flower, over its head

peacock butterfly (PEE kahk BUH tur fly) a butterfly that lives in hollow trees or buildings during the winter

pike (pyk) a large, mean fish that

hunts and eats other fish

piranha (pih RAHN yuh) a small river fish from South America that attacks and eats animals when they wade or swim in the river

plague (PLAYG) another name for a swarm of insects

poisonous (POY suhn uhs) causing sickness or death by poison

prawn (prawhn) a small shrimp-like crustacean

puffer fish (PUH fur fihsh) a fish that can blow up its body like a balloon

pupa (PYOO puh) the case in which a caterpillar changes into an adult

reed frog (reed frawg) a frog that blows up its throat like a balloon when it sings

reptile (REHP tyl) a cold-blooded animal that has dry skin with scales and uses lungs to breathe

salamander (SA luh MAN dur) an amphibian that looks like a lizard with a long tail but has damp skin

scorpion (SKAWR pee uhn) a small invertebrate with claws like a lobster and a poisonous sting on its tail

sea anemone (see uh NEHM uh nee) a soft-bodied sea animal that uses its tentacles to catch food

seahorse (see HAWRS) a fish that has a head like a horse

shark (shahrk) a large, mean fish with sharp teeth

shell (shehl) a hard outer covering

shellfish (SHEHL fihsh) a sea animal with a shell

shingle-back lizard (SHING'L bahk LIH zahrd) a fat lizard with a colorful tongue and mouth

shrimp (shrihmp) a crustacean that looks like a tiny lobster

simple animal (sihm p'l AH nih muhl) an animal without a backbone; also called an invertebrate

skeleton (SKEH leh tuhn) the bone structure of an animal

slug (sluhg) a simple animal that likes wet, cool, shady areas

snail (snayl) a simple animal that hides in its shell to keep cool

snake (snayk) a long, thin reptile without legs

spider (spy dur) an invertebrate with a round body and eight legs

sponge (spuhng) a soft-bodied sea animal

squid (skwihd) a mollusk with 10 arms and no shell

surgeon fish (SUR juhn fihsh) a

coral reef fish with sharp bones near its tail that can cut like a surgeon's knife

swallowtail (SWAHW loh tayl) a butterfly with large, beautiful wings

swarm (swahrm) a large group of insects

swimmerets (SWIH mur ehts) the tiny legs on a lobster

tadpole (TAD pohl) a baby frog

tentacle (TEN tuh k'l) the slender leg or arm of certain animals

termite (TUR myt) an insect that lives in a nest made of earth and eats wood

terrapin (TEHR uh pihn) a small turtle that lives in ponds and rivers and is often kept as a pet

thorax (THAHR ehx) the middle part of an insect's body

toad (tohd) an amphibian with rough skin and no tail

topshell (TAWP shehl) a mollusk with a shell; it crawls around on rocks

tortoise (TAWR tus) a reptile with a hard shell that lives on land

trout (trowt) a river fish that eats insects

tuatara (*TOO* ah *TAHR* ah) a reptile that looks like a lizard

turtle (TUR t'l) a reptile with a hard shell that lives in the water

vertebrae (VUR tuh bray) the rows of bones in a backbone

vertebrate (VUR tuh brayt) an animal with a backbone

warm-blooded (WAWRM bluhd ihd) having blood that stays at almost the same temperature, even when the temperature of the air or other surroundings changes

wasp (wahsp) an insect that lives in a nest and has a sting on its tail

water beetle (WAH tuhr beet'l) a round, flat insect that lives in a pond

water boatman (WAH tuhr BOHT man) a bug that swims on its back and sucks the blood of other animals

winkle (wihn k'l) a mollusk that moves slowly and has a hard shell

worm (wurm) a simple animal with a long, soft body and no legs

FURTHER READING

Bason, Lillian. *Spiders*. Washington: National Geographic Society, 1974. 32pp.

Clemons, Elizabeth. *Tide Pools and Beaches*. New York: Knopf, 1964. 78pp.

Conklin, Gladys. *Insects Build Their Homes*. New York: Holiday House, 1972. 44pp.

Dallinger, Jane. *Frogs and Toads*. Minneapolis: Lerner Publications, 1982.

Dallinger, Jane. *Spiders*. Minneapolis: Lerner Publications, 1981.

Dixon, Dougal. *Prehistoric Reptiles*. New York: Gloucester Press, 1984.

Fields, Alice. *Insects*. New York: F. Watts, 1980.

Gross, Ruth Belov. *Snakes*. New York: Four Winds Press, 1975. 63pp.

Harris, Susan. *Reptiles*. New York: F. Watts, 1978. 48pp.

Hogan, Paula Z. *The Life Cycle of the Butterfly*. Milwaukee: Raintree Childrens Books, 1979.

Hogan, Paula Z. *The Life Cycle of the Crocodile*. Milwaukee: Raintree Childrens Books, 1979.

Hogan, Paula Z. *The Life Cycle of the Frog*. Milwaukee: Raintree Childrens Books, 1979.

Hogan, Paula Z. *The Life Cycle of the Honeybee*. Milwaukee: Raintree Childrens Books, 1979.

Hornblow, Leonora, *Reptiles Do the Strangest Things*. New York: Random House, 1970. 60pp.

Horton, Casey. *Insects*. New York: Gloucester Press, 1983.

Hutchins, Ross. *The Bug Clan*. New York:

Dodd, Mead, 1973. 127pp.

Lambert, David. *Reptiles.* New York: Gloucester Press, 1983.

Lambert, David. *Seashore.* New York: Warwick Press, 1978. 44pp.

Leen, Nina. *Snakes.* New York: Holt, Rinehart and Winston, 1978. 80pp.

McClung, Robert M. *Bees, Wasps and Hornets and How They Live.* New York: Morrow, 1971. 64pp.

Moulton, Robert R. *First to Fly.* Minneapolis: Lerner Publications, 1983.

Overbeck, Cynthia. *Dragonflies.* Minneapolis: Lerner Publications, 1982.

Patent, Dorothy Hinshaw. *Frogs, Toads, Salamanders and How They Reproduce.* New York: Holiday House, 1975. 142pp.

Patent, Dorothy Hinshaw. *How Insects Communicate.* New York: Holiday House, 1975. 127pp.

Patent, Dorothy Hinshaw. *Reptiles and How They Reproduce.* New York: Holiday House, 1977. 127pp.

Reidel, Marlene. *From Egg to Butterfly.* Minneapolis: Carolrhoda Books, 1981.

Selsam, Millicent E. *A First Look at Animals Without Backbones.* New York: Walker, 1976. 32pp.

Selsam, Millicent E. *A First Look at Frogs, Toads and Salamanders.* New York: Walker, 1976. 32pp.

Selsam, Millicent E. *A First Look at Snakes, Lizards and Other Reptiles.* New York: Walker, 1975.

Simon, Hilda. *Insect Masquerades*. New York: Viking Press, 1968. 95pp.

Simon, Hilda. *Snakes: the Facts and the Folklore*. New York: Viking Press, 1973. 128pp.

Stephens, William M. *Come with Me to the Edge of the Sea*. New York: Messner, 1972. 80pp.

Stidworthy, John. *Snakes of the World*. New York: Grosset and Dunlap, 1974. 160pp.

Stonehouse, Bernard. *A Closer Look at Reptiles*. New York: Gloucester Press, 1979. 31pp.

Vevers, Henry Gwynne. *Octopus, Cuttlefish and Squid*. New York: McGraw-Hill, 1977. 48pp.

Victor, Joan Berg. *Shells Are Skeletons*. New York: Crowell, 1977. 33pp.

Wakeman, Norman H. *Wonders of the World Between the Tides*. New York: Dodd, Mead, 1961.

Walther, Tom. *A Spider Might*. San Francisco: Sierra Club Books, 1978. 144pp.

White, William. *Edge of the Ocean*. New York: Sterling Pub. Company, 1977. 80pp.

Zappler, Georg and Lisbeth Zappler. *Amphibians as Pets*. Garden City, New York: Doubleday, 1973. 159pp.

QUESTIONS TO THINK ABOUT

Cold-Blooded Animals

Do you remember?

What are the two main groups of animals called?

If an animal's temperature always stays the same, to what group does it belong?

If an animal's temperature matches the temperature of its surroundings, to what group does the animal belong?

Find out about . . .

How warm-blooded animals in cold climates keep from freezing to death. What kind of body covering do they have? How do they keep from starving? What do bears do to stay alive in winter? What do many kinds of birds do when winter comes? How do beavers get through the winter?

How cold-blooded animals stay alive in very hot or cold seasons. How do frogs and toads keep from freezing to death in winter? How do snakes keep from burning up in a hot desert? What do they do at night?

Animal migration. Why do birds fly south in autumn and north in spring? Do tropical birds migrate? Do whales migrate? If so, why?

Simple Animals

Do you remember?

What is a vertebrate?

How is a simple animal different from a vertebrate?

How does a sea anemone use its tentacles?

What is the body of a sponge made of?

Many simple animals live in our gardens. Name four of them.

Octopuses and squids are mollusks. What kind of bodies do mollusks have?

Find out about . . .

The sea anemone. Why is it called "anemone"? What is an anemone? Is this a good name for this simple animal?

Starfish. What do they eat? Why do fishermen not like starfish?

Octopuses. How does an octopus use its arms? Do the suckers on the arms help the animal in any way?

The squid. How does it move? Why does it squirt water?

Animals with Many Legs

Do you remember?

How many legs does a spider have? Is this more, or less, than the number of legs an insect has?

What is a centipede? How many legs does it have?

What is a millipede? How many legs does it have?

How many legs does a worm have? How does it move?

Where do most crabs and lobsters live?

What is a barnacle? Why do some sailors not like barnacles?

What is a scorpion? How does it use its sting?

Find out about . . .

Shrimps. Where do they live? How are they caught? Why are they important?

Spiders. How many kinds of spiders are there? How many kinds are poisonous? What kinds of webs do spiders make? Where do they get the silk for their webs?

Insects

Do you remember?

An insect's body has three parts. Name them.

What does a caterpillar turn into?

What is a chrysalis?

The emperor moth has spots on its wings. How do these spots help the moth?

How can flies hurt you?

What is a termite? What does it eat?

How are swarms of grasshoppers harmful?

What are aphids? Why do gardeners kill them?

How do worker bees help the queen bee?

Find out about . . .

Termites. How do they build their nests? How does the termite colony work? Who does the work? What does the queen do? How are termites harmful?

The water boatman. Where does it live? How does it move? Why is it called "boatman"?

The dragonfly. Where does it hatch from an egg? How does it grow? Who are its enemies?

Fish

Do you remember?

How do fins help a fish?

Do all fish lay eggs?

How do gills help a fish?

How is the shark's skeleton different from the skeletons of other fish?

Where does the moray eel live?

Many fish that live in rivers and lakes are eaten by people. Name three river fish.

Where does the surgeon fish live?

Find out about...

Making an aquarium. What do you need to make an aquarium? What kind of water must you use? What do the fish need? How must you care for an aquarium?

Mermaid purses. What are they? Where are they found?

Sea horses. How are they like other fish? How are they different? Why are they called "horses"? How do they care for their babies?

Amphibians

Do you remember?

Do all amphibians live in wet places?

What is a tadpole?

How does the jelly around a frog's eggs protect those eggs?

Tell three ways that frogs and tadpoles are different.

What are newts? Where do they live?

How is the body of a salamander different from the body of a toad or of a frog?

Find out about...

The tree frog. How big is it? Where does it live? What does it eat? What time of day can you see it? Why can it hide easily from its enemies?

How frogs swim. What kind of stroke do they use? Do they spend much time in water?

The reed frog. Why does it blow up like a balloon when it sings? Is its body different in ~~any way~~ from the bodies of other frogs?

Reptiles

Do you remember?

How does the Australian rock python protect its eggs from enemies?

Do all snakes lay eggs?

Do all lizards have four legs?

Where do crocodiles live? What do they eat?

What is a tortoise? How does it grow? How does it move? How does it protect itself?

Why do sea turtles come to shore?

Why can snakes swallow large animals?

Find out about . . .

Ancient reptiles. When did the dinosaurs live? How many kinds of dinosaurs were there? How small was the smallest? How large was the biggest one? How do we know that dinosaurs actually lived on earth? Why can't we see dinosaurs now?

Fire salamanders. How did the false story about this animal's ability to stand fire get started?

Poisonous snakes. Which kinds of snakes are poisonous? What is a pit viper?

Attack and Defense

Do you remember?

When do bees and wasps sting?

What happens when a honeybee stings you? Why does the sting hurt?

Why can animals that suck blood be dangerous to people?

What is malaria? How is it spread?

What is a piranha? Why is it dangerous to cattle and other animals?

Find out about . . .

Jellyfish. How do they get their food? Do they attack people?

Leeches. Why were these animals once used by doctors? Where do leeches live?

The stick insect. What does it look like? What does it eat? Where does it live? How big is it?

PROJECTS

Project — Warm-blooded and Cold-blooded Animals

Find as many old magazines and newspapers as you can. Search through each one for pictures of animals. If the name of the animal is given, write this name on a slip of paper. Then pin the slip on the picture. You should find at least ten pictures for this project.

You will also need two pieces of poster board. Across the top of one board, print the words "Cold-blooded Animals." Color this board blue. Across the top of the other board, print "Warm-blooded Animals." Color this board pink. You are now ready to sort and paste your pictures.

Separate the pictures of all the animals you think are cold-blooded. Paste them on the blue board. Write the name of the animal under each picture. Paste the pictures of all the warm-blooded animals on the pink board. Write the name of the animal under each picture. If you do not know the name of an animal, use library books to help you find out.

Project — Animal Differences

Show with drawings how some animals are different from each other. Draw these pairs: a snake and a lizard; a lobster and a shrimp or prawn; a spider and a beetle; a fish and a frog; a snail and a turtle.

INDEX

Alligators 57
Amphibians 48-53
Ants 10, 11, 36-37
Aphids 10, 34, 35
Barnacles 12, 13, 20-21
Bees 7, 36-37, 62
Beetles 7, 30, 34-35
Bugs 7, 34-35
Butterflies 7, 11, 24-25, 26-27
Caddisflies 30
Caterpillars 24-25
Centipedes 17
Crabs 7, 8, 17, 18-19
Crickets 32-33
Crocodiles 6, 57
Dragonflies 30
Fish 6, 7, 12, 13, 38-47, 63
Flies 22-23, 28-29
Frogs 6, 48-49, 50-51
Grasshoppers 32-33
Insects 24-37
Jellyfish 6, 62
Ladybugs 10, 11, 35
Lizards 7, 55, 56
Lobsters 18-19
Locusts 32-33
Millipedes 17
Monkeys 7, 17
Mosquitoes 28, 63
Moths 11, 24-25, 26
Newts 52-53
Octopuses 6, 14
Ponds 30
Prawns 12

Reptiles 54-61
Rock pools 12-13, 18, 21
Salamanders 52-53
Scorpions 7, 22
Sea anemones 6, 9, 12, 13
Shellfish 13
Shrimps 7, 20-21
Skeletons 8-9
Slugs 10
Snails 6, 10, 11, 16
Snakes 7, 54, 60-61, 62
Spiders 7, 10, 11, 17, 22-23
Sponges 6, 9
Squids 14-15
Starfish 6, 13
Terrapins 59
Termites 31
Toads 50
Tortoises 6, 58-59
Tuataras 55
Turtles 58-59
Wasps 36, 62
Water boatmen 30, 35
Worms, 6, 8, 10, 11, 16

Photo Credits: Andrea; Biofotos/H. Angel; Bruce Coleman; Jeff Goodman; Alan Hutchison; A.G. Leutscher; Natural History Photography Agency; S. Walker.

Front cover: Milwaukee Public Museum/Photographic Collection.

Illustrators: Barbara Bailey; John Barber; Richard Eastland; Gill Embleton; Vanessa Luff; Stephanie Manchipp; Sean Rudman; George Thompson; Mike Whelply.